Visionistics

The Process of Success

Nolan W. Burris

Published by Visionistics Enterprises, Inc.
Vancouver, BC, Canada

Publisher: Visionistics Enterprises, Inc.

ISBN: 978-0-9809332-0-8

1st edition, July 2009

Contact information:
Visionistics Enterprises, Inc.
visionistics.com
Email: info@visionistics.com

Table Of Contents

Friends, family, coworkers and complete strangers are all part of the infinite and often unknown connections that bring your dreams and theirs to life.

Acknowledgements

The Helping part

It would be impossible to acknowledge all the incredible people who have contributed to the creation of this book and the ideas behind it. The dream of the book is one I have carried in my heart for many years. Without the help and support of some very dear friends and cherished family members it would not have become a reality.

Please know that you are all loved and appreciated. To Carol, your assistance and friendship are both priceless. To my mother Nanka, you have always inspired and motivated me in countless ways. Where would I be without you? Casper, you leave me in awe with your love, devotion and undying belief that anything is possible.

I offer special thanks to Mike Marchev. During a speaking engagement where we shared the stage Mike made a bet that changed everything for me. He asked me when I thought I could finally turn my ideas into the book I had been dreaming about for so long. I tossed out *"two months with no distractions."* He then wagered $1,000 that I couldn't do it. Of course what he really meant was *"sure you can."* Thirty days later, the book was complete.

Thanks Mike for taking me from a bet to a dream fulfilled. I hope this book will in some way inspire others to transform their own dreams into reality.

Satisfaction is not the final step in the journey. It is the joy that propels you into the next, and the next, and the next.

Introduction

The Starting Part

Over the years I have met some truly remarkable people. I have known simple, peaceful, spiritual masters and charismatic leaders. I have had the privilege to work for brilliant businesspeople and for some very special companies. I have also encountered countless ordinary people doing extraordinary things with their own lives and for others. With them I have felt joy and excitement, disappointment, love and sadness - ultimately learning something wonderful from every experience.

When my own life was out of sync with the dreams I felt inside I turned to those who lived their dreams every day. When I experienced personal triumphs and successes I was reminded of the things I had learned from some of the wisest people I had ever met. Some of these sages have flitted in and out of my life in a flash. Others are near permanent fixtures in my daily routine. The amount of time spent together has never been a measurement for the quality of love and kindness that occurred.

Through it all one thing has become undeniably clear to me: we are surrounded by infinite opportunities to learn and to serve every day. A simple walk down the street can have you brushing shoulders with present-day strangers that hold the potential to be future partners in the creation of a dream. I have learned that often times we need only open our eyes, our ears, and our hearts to reach out into that sea of possibilities.

It is equally important that while we are reaching with a taking hand we are also reaching with one that is giving back. Your dreams and the dreams of those around you are more interdependent than we may ever know. Specific knowledge of how they interconnect is unimportant. Just understand that any dream you have is only going to happen through the participation of others. You have to be an active part of the team for any real personal victories to take place.

If a dream lives only in your heart, it isn't likely to come true. If it never lives in your heart, it doesn't stand a chance.

Vision

The Feeling Part

There is the kind of vision that involves your eyes, and there is the kind that involves your heart. While the former may help you navigate your surroundings, it is the latter that can help you navigate toward your future. That kind of vision is more powerful than a dream alone, more meaningful than fantasy, and more potent than logic. It is also fundamental in creating and sustaining success and happiness.

Vision is the common thread connecting great leaders to ordinary people who are extraordinarily happy. It is a fire of passion that burns with such intensity as to extinguish impossibility.

It is available to anyone who is willing to look beyond what is and look instead toward what can be. It is always available in limitless quantities for an infinite number of desires of countless types.

From minor achievements to monumental transformations, vision is the first step toward manifestation. It is an expression of something deep inside. It is something that may have started as a daydream or fantasy, but has picked up steam and is hurtling toward reality. It is an idea with emotional energy behind it. It is an idea with feeling. It is a feeling that spills over the boundaries of imagination and reaches into the physical world.

Have you ever heard the expression *"I'm so excited I can almost taste it"*? That's what happens when a thought or idea gets mixed with the future-shaping punch of emotions. It is a dream that is so real, so strongly desired, that you begin to feel it long before it emerges into real life. That's the kind of vision that produces success and happiness of the highest order.

The Reverend Dr. Martin Luther King proclaimed: *"I have a dream,"* with the conviction of every cell in his body. He used the word dream, but it was clearly more than a flight of fancy. He felt it with such strength and such commitment that nothing could sway him. It was a vision that burned within his heart and radiated out to everyone around him. He moved people with his very presence. That's the kind of vision that changes the world.

The incredibly successful businessman and well-known philanthropist Bill Gates once said: *"Microsoft was founded with a vision of a computer on every desk, and in every home. We've never waivered from that vision."* He had the vision long before most people believed it was possible or even feasible. He had it before most people had ever touched a computer. He was dreaming about it. He was feeling it. He was *"tasting"* it. He completely believed it. That's the kind of vision that revolutionizes business.

Do you have a vision? It doesn't have to be as world changing as equality for all humanity or as complex as technological innovation. It also doesn't have to be singular.

Most people have many different desires in life. Some are probably more important to you than others. Some may be nothing more than fun fantasies, with very little desire to actually make them real. Some might be so strong that, like Bill Gates, you can *"almost taste it."* Which ones do you think are most likely to become real?

Why aren't more people making their own dreams come true? If vision has so much potential for sparking the flames of change, you might wonder why more people aren't using it, talking about it and, living the life they always wanted. There are at least three reasons: (1) they think it's impossible; (2) they don't know how; and (3) they haven't really thought about it. Correction: They haven't really FELT about it.

It's normal to daydream. It's normal to fantasize. It's also normal to make things happen, to create and to change things. Change is the nature of the entire universe.

Nothing in the universe is still or motionless. Atoms are furiously flying around within the most seemingly solid objects that exist. Even doing nothing is actually still doing something!

Why does this matter? Because tapping into the supercharged power of vision is almost as easy as doing nothing. You won't have to lift a finger. You will have to open your heart and your mind. You will have to feel. You may also have to let go of your own self-imposed barriers of disbelief.

Not too many years ago the idea of developing a mission statement took hold in the corporate world. It is still considered by many to be a critical element of proper business planning. Some bankers even require it before approving a company for financing. There's a good reason for such requirements. A mission statement is intended to be a thoughtful and succinct declaration of the primary objectives of an organization. It is assumed to be more than just a goal. A mission statement is supposed to be the driving motivation behind the very existence of the business.

Having a mission statement sounds like a pretty good idea for a business, and maybe even for an individual as well. Curiously, most businesses don't have one. Even among those that do, there's a problem. Many mission statements have devolved into promotional opportunities that have lost their original intent.

While there are certainly exceptions, it seems that a lot of mission statements are crafted within corporate marketing departments as a result of demographic studies and for advertising purposes. From a purely fiscal point of view, there can be some value in such endeavors, but they are missing the most important ingredient of all: passion.

Passion is the power behind Bill Gates'

many pursuits and passion drove the Reverend King to inspire millions. Passion is the meaning behind the words. It is the substance and the foundation below the surface. Without passion, a mission statement is just a pleasant-sounding group of words.

Somewhere, at some point in time, the founders of nearly every successful company had a vision for what they wanted to create or do. Sometimes, with some people or companies, the passion gets lost along the way. Sometimes it gets reignited in the hearts of those who follow. Sometimes the details get in the way and extinguish the passion that was reignited or once burned so brightly.

Things change. Details matter. Right? Well, maybe not so much when it comes to vision. There is a common trait among great visionaries: they don't let the details distract them. Details are important, but their job is to support the manifestation of the vision, not to derail it.

Great visionaries also don't let the winds of change blow them entirely off course. These factors, change and details, are the two most vulnerable points for keeping a vision alive.

How often do you find yourself explaining away a dream before it ever gets a fighting chance? How often do you say, *"Yeah, but..."* and begin to focus more on the *"how"* than the *"why?"*

We've all done it with something. Most of the time, it's not a big deal. But when it comes to achieving your life's passions, it is a very big deal.

How often have you said something like this: *"Well, it was a great idea at the time, but things have changed since then."* Thus letting the idea fade into history? Change is inevitable. A vision—a passionate vision—should be strong enough, and with enough commitment behind it, to withstand the change that will certainly swirl around it at all times.

Of course, some people have no vision at all. When asked what they want out of life, they may be hard-pressed to give a deep and meaningful answer.

There is one vision though, that can fit the bill for everyone. So, if you find yourself struggling to articulate or define what your own personal vision might be, try this one on for size: to be happy.

Strategies

Vision  Ethics

Tactics

Howard's Story
Part One

A number of years ago I was speaking at an event in Chicago when I met an unassuming man named Howard (not his real name). I had just addressed the audience on the power of integrity and ethics in business and in life. It's a subject I frequently speak about, and one in which I strongly believe.

Howard approached me after my presentation to tell me about his business. He was the owner of a small but growing travel agency that specialized in adventure and eco-related trips. I was immediately intrigued as I am a big fan of adventure travel in particular. I asked him how he got started in the travel business. He responded with a very moving and inspiring story.

He told me that in 1986 he spent his vacation in Costa Rica. Having grown up in the city of Chicago, he was interested in taking in some natural beauty and seeing a rainforest.

Howard was not really a typical adventure seeker. He said he wanted to expand his experiences by trying something new and a little outside of his self-described comfort zone.

As he told me about his trip, it became obvious that this vacation had transformed into something much bigger. He spoke of seeing vast mountains greener than he had ever seen. He described the smell of roasting coffee beans he had picked with his own hands.

He relived the moment he saw monkeys in the wild. He tried to explain the feeling of taking in a deep long breath of the cleanest air he had ever breathed, while standing in the middle of a damp verdant rainforest. *"Somehow"* he said, *"you just can't fully explain it."*

Howard told me that he was completely changed by that trip. He said that in a flash, he knew what he wanted to do with the rest of his life, he just didn't know how. Howard's vision was born years after he thought he had chosen his personal and professional path.

His vision lived only in his heart for three years after the trip. During those three years, his vision grew stronger and became more defined. It evolved from a feeling into a desire—something he *"could almost taste."* He finally took a leap of faith, changed careers, and bought a small, failing travel agency.

Howard's vision was so meaningful to him that he eventually had it printed on the back of his business cards, on a poster in his office, and at the bottom of every customer invoice. This is what it said:

"In 1986 I took a trip to Costa Rica for the very first time. I breathed air cleaner than I thought existed and I saw natural beauty I had never imagined. I knew that if I could show others what I had seen, we just might take better care of the planet we call home. This travel agency is my way of sharing the magic I discovered back in 1986."

Your Vision

Write down something that lives in your heart. Look for something that when fully realized will bring you joy and satisfaction.

_____

_____

_____

_____

_____

_____

_____

_____

_____

_____

Your heart is the incubator of your dreams. Your mind is the factory of your plans. Your passion is the power that keeps both in good operating order.

Strategies

The Thinking Part

Visions are born in your heart. So are dreams. So are fantasies. It's those dreams and fantasies that take on some special meaning or importance that become our visions.

The emotional center of our being is our personal power plant of creation. But if your visions only live in your heart, they will either burn up and evaporate, or slowly eat away at your sense of fulfillment and purpose. A vision is a dream that has become so important to us that it leaps from our hearts and into our heads. That's when manifestation into reality begins to take shape. Emotion is energy but logic is direction.

Vision is the feeling part of your journey and strategies are the thinking part. If vision is the fuel, then strategies represent the route. The analogy of planning a driving trip is quite appropriate when considering the strategic side of creating your vision.

We are all on a journey. Some of us are on a well-planned conscious journey of passion. Some of us are just bumbling along with no particular destination in mind. Either way, without fuel you won't get very far very fast. Without a route and a plan, you'll run out of fuel long before you even get close to the destination.

It's amazing how often we say out loud that we *"really want something"* but do virtually nothing to set the wheels in motion. Strategies are the wheels and vision provides the motion.

To take the driving trip analogy just a bit further, think about the wheels on your car. There's actually a little more connected to the axles than just wheels. You'll also find the right kind of hub and the right kind of lug nuts and the right kind of tires with the right kind of tread.   Each part was specifically chosen to support and propel the vehicle for which they were selected. Put another way, they were chosen strategically.

Strategies are those big picture plans used to make your goals and dreams come true. Strategies, similar to vision, shouldn't be bogged down with too many details, but they should be well designed and carefully considered. While the above example of wheels on a car may seem like a lot of details, it's really about being consciously selective. It's about taking each piece and weighing it against it's potential to take you closer to your vision.

For example, all-weather tires might be a great strategy for a car that only rarely encounters icy roads. For one that is regularly in frozen climates winter tires would be the logical choice. The worst choice would be to simply not give it any thought at all! Strategies are the thinking part. The thinking that should be taking place is all about laying the groundwork to bring the vision to life.

If you wanted to become a brain surgeon, you would have to go medical school. To go to medical school you would have to do fairly well in the right courses in college. To do well in the right courses in college you would have to strategically select the right courses. While there are probably brilliant surgeons who first majored in literature, they eventually had to make a strategic change of course to get on the brilliant surgeon path. That change of direction was called for by the emergence of a vision – the vision to be a surgeon.

Can your vision change? Of course! Think about how many youngsters dream of becoming fire fighters, astronauts, and movie stars. Now, think about how many fire fighters, astronauts and movie stars there are. While their numbers aren't limitless, clearly lots of people did it! Some may have had that vision in their hearts as long as they could remember. For some it was a fluke or a twist of fate. Most of us had to try on a few different visions over the years before we found the right fit and some of us are still searching.

How do you know if you've found the right fit? You feel it. You want it. You begin to experience the joy and the sensations of it being real long before it can be touched or seen by others. It starts to take shape in the imagination of your heart. If you feed it and give it more of your passion and more of your energy it will eventually spread from your heart to take up residence in your head. That's when it's time to let logic start working it's magic.

Logic by definition is a thought process. It is step-by-step reasoning to solve a problem. In terms of achieving your vision, think of it as creating the most direct or meaningful path. To once again use the driving analogy, you might think that taking an expressway would be the most expedient route to your destination, but the local roads could show you more interesting sights along the way.

The challenge is really just a decision about which is more important to you: getting to the destination faster or exploring the local sights.

This is the sort of challenge we face every day in our own journeys. With the vision as our destination there will be countless opportunities to get off the expressway and experience the sights along the way. In some ways, those side trips may even enhance and strengthen the vision. That is, if they are selected strategically. There is however, a big difference between enhancement, distraction, and total redirection. Always be mindful of the type and purpose of side trip you are taking.

Visionistics is a simple approach to achieving your vision. If you already have a vision, or even several of them, then the first step is done but should never be forgotten. Do you still feel it? Does it still burn like a fire? Is it pushing outward from within you with such power that your chest is tight with anticipation? Is it still so strong that you can almost taste it? That's when it's time to start thinking strategically. That's when it's time to start putting plans into place. It's time to pull out the map and trace the route.

You should strategically allow for side trips, construction delays and heavy traffic. You should also strategically select those that will strengthen your vision and avoid those that will dilute or distract from it.

It is simply a matter of time and priority. How much time will you spend on things that are either completely unrelated to your vision or worse, at odds with it? Some of that is to be expected, but before the fuel runs out you need to get back on course. Before the clock runs out you must be ever aware of the minutes and hours that are forever lost to things that are not part of your vision.

It's not about being single minded, but about being conscious and aware. Forgive yourself for any past mistakes and use them as reminders for future decisions. Strategies are the plans, decisions and choices that take you further away from or closer to making your vision a reality. Every choice is yet another step on the path. One wrong step is easily corrected. Many wrong steps are harder. All of them are more easily accomplished when your vision is clear in your mind and in your heart.

Strategies

Vision   Ethics

Tactics

Howard's Story

Part Two

Howard's vision of sharing the magic of planet earth with others was clear. His first strategy for making it happen was put in motion when he bought the travel agency. He felt that he could attract others who shared his vision by specializing in and promoting eco-related trips.

Adventure travel quickly became another part of the strategy when he discovered that things like white water rafting, bungee jumping, zip lining and hang gliding often took place in the very areas he wanted people to see. That's when he encountered his first strategic dilemma.

It seemed that while many eco and adventure travel wholesalers were indeed in alignment with his vision, others were not so holistically supportive. He told me that some well-known eco tour providers were owned or operated by corporations that also had other endeavors that were unacceptable to him.

There were for example, companies that built or managed resorts in ecologically sensitive or endangered areas. While this may not be an issue for many people, it was in direct opposition to Howard's vision. He strongly believed that he could only support tour providers that shared his long-term view.

Seemingly speaking from a purely business-like perspective Howard said, *"There won't be much eco travel to sell if they eventually burn down all the rainforests to build resorts."*

But his vision was more than just a perspective on business; it was his personal conviction.   He then made his second strategic decision: to only support and sell those eco and adventure travel providers that supported their local economies and were committed to preserving the natural beauty in which they operated.

I was enthralled by Howard's passion and commitment to his vision. I was also very impressed with the seemingly natural selection of strategies to get there. I noticed however that something was troubling him. Somewhere something was threatening his vision. I saw the expression on his face change from joy and excitement to one of concern and stress. The real reason Howard approached me was just beginning to emerge.

The average person spends eight hours a day sleeping, eight working, one getting to and from work, and two for meals and preparation. Of the five hours remaining, most people spend four and a half of them watching television. That doesn't leave much time to make your dreams come true.

Your Strategies

Now, take your vision and think logically. Think of *"big picture"* ways to bring your vision closer to reality and to keep it alive. Take note of other strategic issues that may be in opposition to your vision. Can they be changed or eliminated?

_____

_____

_____

_____

_____

_____

_____

_____

_____

What are dreams but your innermost desire to do more than you have done so far? Why rationalize them away until you've explored them to their fullest potential? Instead, use your rational thought to make sense out of fantasy.

Tactics

The Doing Part

If vision lives in your heart, and strategies live in your head, tactics would live in your hands. Vision is the feeling part. Strategies are the thinking part. Tactics are the doing part. They are the convergence of emotion and logic into physical manifestation. They represent the point where you move beyond feeling and thinking and actually start doing!

This seemingly obvious step in bringing your vision to life is perhaps not so obvious upon closer inspection. Think about all the great ideas you've had in your own life. Think about those you've heard about from family, friends and colleagues.

From get-rich schemes and world changing concepts to plans for repainting the living room, it seems that ideas are seldom in short supply. It's putting the plans into action and picking up the paintbrush that appears to be the hard part.

There is no shortage of reasons and excuses for a lack of action: *"There's too little time and too much to do." "I've just been too busy." "Something else came up." "Our budget no longer allows for such endeavors." "Our corporate policy has changed."*

Regardless of the reason, or the excuse, the end result is the same: it didn't get done.
If you don't get around to repainting the living room, it's an annoying disappointment. If you don't get around to bringing a passionate vision to life, it's a terrible tragedy. It's a tragedy that can be avoided.

Vision is an emotional feeling that is born in your heart. Strategies are logical thought processes that come from your mind. Tactics, while mostly about getting things done, aren't however, entirely physical in nature.

In the military, a tactical exercise is not a random free-for-all of shooting here and there. It is a very specific set of activities designed to support a very specific strategy. In other words, it is not just getting things done, but taking the right steps at the right time and in the right direction to stay in alignment with the strategic plan. If the strategic plan is continually kept in alignment with the objectives (the vision), then a successful tactical maneuver will result, thus moving another step closer to the final objective.

What does all of this have to do with

achieving your own vision? Plenty! Let's assume that one of your visions is to live a mostly debt-free life. Perhaps your strategic plan to get there involves finding lower interest options to refinance existing debt, doubling the minimum payments required, and paying for all future purchases with cash.

It sounds like a great strategy – if you do it. If however, you choose to watch an old sitcom rerun instead of researching lower interest options, you have placed yourself at a tactical disadvantage. If you then order a shiny new thingamajig advertised during the commercials – where only credit cards are accepted – you've made yet another tactical misstep.

If making the purchase requires raising your credit limit a smidge another tactical error is at hand. When the new higher balance on your account causes your minimum payment to rise to the previously planned double payments then the resulting tactical pileup will be in nearly complete opposition to the strategies for which they were intended.

As with strategies, tactics are not about being single-minded or avoiding the occasional pleasurable distraction. There are two very important words in that last sentence: *distraction and pleasurable*.

If your vision doesn't bring you as much pleasure and joy as the distractions that will mostly certainly surround you most of the time then perhaps it isn't a vision that has fully matured in the incubator of your heart.

Maybe you're not really ready to unleash it from your emotional center. Maybe it doesn't have enough commitment behind it to take advantage of the power of logic. Or, maybe you just need to reconnect with why you had the vision in the first place.

Reigniting the passion behind your vision is just like changing the oil in your car. If you don't do it regularly something is going to give out or burn up. Grinding gears and other noises can even tempt you to abandon the vision entirely in search of a new one.

Sometimes, that might be the perfect thing to do. Things change. Desires change. Life changes. That being said; don't be too quick to give up on or dismiss the old jalopy without first reexamining why you chose it. After all, a new vision requires new strategies and new tactics, which could lead you into a perpetual state of starting over.

For some people, this can be a never-ending cycle with unfulfilling and exhausting consequences. But, it can also be quite seductive. Newness can be much more attractive to some than sameness.

Some of us fear new and different things. Some of us thrive on new and different. Either way a passionate vision is something that can rise above fear and outshine difference. A truly passionate vision that you can *"almost taste"* rarely vanishes completely. Somewhere deep inside a spark of the original fire is waiting to be refueled perhaps even to a degree greater and stronger and with more definition than before. Before you let it go, isn't it worth feeling it again? Isn't it worth *"tasting"* it again?

Day by day with every decision we make, both big and small, we are moving closer to or further away from our vision. Staying aware and making conscious choices about each decision you face is the tactical approach to realizing your dreams. This applies to distractions as well. None of us are superhuman. We need rest and recovery time. Barreling toward your vision at full throttle at all times may get you there faster, but you might be too exhausted to enjoy the satisfaction! Choose your distractions as well as you choose your tactics and you'll be far more likely to stick to your vision.

Actively seek things that are restful and enjoyable but complimentary to your vision. Spending time on things that do not directly contribute to your vision is fine! It could be just the thing you need to reinvigorate a tired vision. It all depends on how the time is spent.

Neutral time can be very refreshing. Negative time on the other hand, will deplete your resources. So, avoid things that are contrary to or at odds with your vision. At the very least, choose those things wisely with full knowledge that you'll have to make up for the loss if you want to stay on track.

If your vision depends on other people, as is the case in most business situations, be aware that those other people are your tactical soldiers in the field. While they may unquestioningly follow any order given, it is those who truly understand the strategy behind the order that will execute it in a way that better supports the objective.

Those who understand the vision will follow it with something even more powerful: passion. Of course, in a business or team, it isn't always possible to share the same vision as the leader; at least not in as meaningful a way as the originator of the vision. But, something very special happens when you speak from your heart.

When you speak from your heart the words get mixed with the energy of the vision. The passion of the vision gives the words more significance and importance. That is not to say that everyone will agree, but at least they may empathize and understand.

Empathy, like passion, is emotional. Emotion is the power that turns visions into reality. If your vision depends on other people, those other people depend on your passion to help you create your vision.

Tactics are a physical act. By adding the direction of logic and the fuel of emotion you can help keep each tactical step more closely aligned with the manifestation of the vision.

Strategies

Vision · Ethics

Tactics

Howard's Story

Part Three

Howard was distressed. He had described to me a beautiful and inspiring story of a man on a quest to live his dream. He had shared some of his key strategies for not only making it happen but for keeping it alive and well. I was confused by his sudden change of mood. Something was amiss.

"I have a problem," he said. *"This is my third year in business. It's a critical time when we are shifting from loss to profit and from investment to payback."* At this point, while I did not yet know the specifics Howard was facing, I was fairly certain it was a money problem. Then, Howard surprised me.

"I just received a bonus check for almost $10,000." *"Howard,"* I said, *"that doesn't seem like a problem to me!"* Howard explained that like most travel agents, he earned his income through a combination of professional consulting fees from clients and commissions paid by the tour operators whose packages he sold.

Sometimes, when a travel agency has exceptionally high sales with a particular tour operator, they receive bonus payments called overrides. Such was the case with the money Howard had just received. He had been carrying the check in his wallet for almost two weeks.

"It seems to me that you're doing something right since not every travel agency gets that kind of bonus" I said with a congratulatory smile on my face. *"Yes,"* said Howard, *"but we did something wrong that resulted in this check and that's the real problem."*

I had trouble imagining what the wrong thing was that could cause Howard to carry the check in his wallet for so long without depositing it into his account. Was it a legal problem? Was it an accounting error? It was in fact a tactical error.

Howard reminded me of his vision of sharing the natural beauty of the world with others. He also reminded me of one of his key strategies: to only support tour operators that shared his long-term vision, protected the areas in which they operated, supported the local economies and such. The check Howard had recently received was from one of the *"wrong"* tour operators!

If Howard's dreams were primarily about

profit, he might have simply deposited the check and stepped $10,000 closer to his vision. While profit was still very important and integral to his overall vision, his driving passion was about something else. The fact that he had not yet deposited the check was clear evidence that he was struggling with the source of the revenue.

"How did this happen?" I asked. *"It sounds like you had a great plan in place."* *"Well,"* he said, *"I had a good plan in place, but it wasn't well executed. I didn't get the word out to the staff."*

Put another way, there was a problem at the tactical level. As it turned out, Howard's highest producing and most talented travel agent believed she was doing the right thing for the company by selling a very popular and well-respected tour operator. It just didn't happen to be a tour operator that was aligned with Howard's vision or strategies. Unfortunately, she didn't know any of that. Her only tactical instructions were to sell.

Up to this point Howard was the sole keeper of the vision. It lived only within his heart and had not been shared with anyone. He had used the magic of logic to create an excellent strategic plan. He had unfortunately failed to ensure that his tactics were in alignment. In other words, the other people responsible for helping him to create the vision were not even aware of it.

So I asked Howard again, *"What is the problem? You haven't deposited the check yet so it appears that you're still thinking about it. I can't tell you if you should or shouldn't deposit the check. I can't tell you if depositing the check compromises your vision. Only you know that. I also don't know your financial circumstances. But I do know this: I know your vision and I will try to repeat back to you as you told it to me."*

I then did my best to repeat Howard's vision back to him:

"In 1986 I took a trip to Costa Rica for the very first time. I breathed air cleaner than I thought existed and I saw natural beauty I had never imagined. I knew that if I could show others what I had seen, we just might take better care of the planet we call home. This travel agency is my way of sharing the magic I discovered back in 1986."

I then said *"Howard, I'm afraid this decision*

is yours and yours alone. Just think about that decision and whether it will take you closer to or further away from your vision. Don't just think about it – feel about it. I'd love to hear what you decide."

We shook hands and said goodbye. What followed was something truly amazing.

Your Tactics

Take one or two of the strategies you created and think about specific steps or actions to implement them. Be mindful of staying in alignment with the strategy for which each tactic is designed and keep your vision as the ultimate objective. Are there any tactical things you are doing now that are in opposition to your vision or strategies?

_____

_____

_____

_____

_____

_____

_____

_____

Your ethics may begin as an internal sense of what is right and what is wrong, but only when they become an external demonstration of the same is their value truly realized.

Ethics

The Guiding Part

By now you know that vision is the first and most significant ingredient in the recipe for success. It is the feeling part that springs from your heart and into your head where strategies, the thinking part get blended in. Tactics are the doing part where your well-blended creation is baked to perfection. Similar to making a cake, it is not just the ingredients and not just the proportions that matter. The way in which they are blended can completely change the final result.

Sometimes the batter is stiff and requires more vigorous stirring. At other times the batter may be smooth and thin where a lighter touch is called for. Drier climates, higher altitudes, different pans and more can all require the baker to make decisions that may alter the originally planned approach.

In the context of Visionistics you might say that the strategic plan of making a cake remains solid but the tactical approach to get there requires the occasional on-the-spot adjustment. From corporate policies to personal financial freedom, the tactical steps along the strategic path will almost certainly require tweaks, changes and decisions in order to keep moving in the direction of the vision. How do you make those decisions?

What guides you in making the tweaks? What is the motivation that drives the direction of the change?

There are knee-jerk reactions from unexpected surprises. Then there is the slow slippage caused by boredom or faded enthusiasm. Surely something can help you make conscious decisions that keep you on track with your vision rather than meandering around quite so much! Ethics are the guiding principles that can give meaning and direction to every decision.

Ethics is a powerful word. It represents integrity, morality, and purity of intent. The subject of ethics can conjure up very big and far-reaching ideas and ideals. Ethics can also represent a very personal and intimate dialogue of very personal and intimate feelings. There is one concept however, that seems to span all of these variations. In its simplest form, ethics are really all about doing the right thing.

In the Visionistics sense of the word, ethics means doing the right thing for your vision. It means using the vision as the weight and balance for every decision about every strategy and tactic. It means returning to the vision before reacting to the winds of change and distraction. It means reconnecting with the vision when the lure of something new or the fear of the unknown competes for your attention.

We may all have a different opinion about the right thing to do for the planet, but when it comes to the right thing to do for your vision opinions are not the answer. If the vision in question is your own personal vision, it is your own personal ethics that should guide you. It is your own sense of what is right and what is wrong for your own personal vision that matters the most.

Ethics represent your own personal guidance system. Like vision, ethics are emotionally based. Ethics live in your heart. You might even say they live in your soul. Guilt and remorse are the emotional results of making a decision that is contrary to your vision.

We all know that feeling. We've all experienced some degree of personal shame when we were not true to ourselves or to others. Guilt, shame or remorse can be very unpleasant yet they each serve an important collective purpose. They let us know when we are off-course and when we did not do the right thing.

When it comes to the vision of a business or organization, the guiding principles of ethics take on a slightly different context. Within any group of people, be it a corporate board meeting or an airline reservation department, each individual brings their own personal ethics along to work with them every day. Even if they have not spent much time defining or thinking about them, something is guiding their actions and reactions to situations they encounter. To think that we can simply switch off our own personal guidance system when we walk through the doors of our place of employment is naïve at best.

This is very important to understand because, every individual's personal decision making criteria will be used by default unless there is a different criteria provided. In the corporate setting, we usually refer to this as a policy manual.

The intent of a policy manual is to anticipate the various situations that may occur and provide a specific, often very specific decision. From specifying the acceptable style of dress to defining the number of rings allowed before answering the telephone, corporate policies anticipate decisions by effectively eliminating them. The decision has been made in advance.

There is an inherent flaw in the policy manual approach to guiding decisions. While some things like wardrobe selection and telephone rings are perfectly placed within the policy manual approach there is something missing. There is something that doesn't fit particularly well within the anticipatory preemptive nature of policies: guiding principles.

It is impossible to anticipate every eventuality. It is impossible to pre-decide everything that may come along for every person on the team. If those people are not given the guiding principles of the organization then they will rely on their own personal principles, which may or may not be even remotely related to the vision of the organization.

Whether you are a corporate executive, a supervisor or just an individual whose vision depends on other people, communicating a set of guiding principles to your team is essential.

In the early 1980s the term *"empowerment"* crept into the corporate vocabulary. The idea behind it was and still is sound: allow your team members to make decisions on their own and efficiency will follow. It's a great idea but without guiding principles those decisions may or may not be in alignment with the vision.

Any employee or team member that is not fully aware of the vision that they are helping to create is like a bullet ricocheting around bouncing off unguided decisions. They may not share the vision with the same feeling and emotional connection as its designer, but they must at least understand it.

The better everyone on a team understands the vision the better their own tactical decisions will be. Giving them guiding principles that are in alignment with the vision will help keep those tactical decisions on course for the strategies they support.

From businesses and charities to regular folks with hopes and dreams, ethics are about being true and loyal to the vision. Any decision that takes you further away from the vision is an ethical misstep of some sort. Any decision that is at odds with a strategy (presumably designed to support the vision) is another potential ethical error in the making. Too many ethical errors result in an ethical collapse that becomes harder and harder from which to recover.

Ethics are your guiding principles that, if adhered to, keep you on course and on track. Yet, it seems very few people and very few businesses have given ethics much thought at all. Is it any wonder then that so many visions and so many dreams simply fade away?

Ethics is doing the right thing. Doing the right thing is an emotional reaction. Vision is an emotional creation. Vision and ethics come from your heart. Strategies come from the logical power of your mind. Tactics are the physical actions to bring it all into reality. Vision is the feeling part. Strategies are the thinking part. Tactics are the doing part. Ethics are the guiding part. When all these are in alignment a very, very powerful thing emerges: integrity.

Integrity is the glue that binds all the elements of vision, strategies, tactics and ethics together. Integrity is a state upon which the ultimate manifestation of the vision is completely dependent. It is the final yet ever changing state of being from which success will blossom into existence.

Strategies

Vision  **Ethics**

Tactics

Howard's Story

Part Four

Howard found himself facing an ethical dilemma. His vision was crystal clear. His strategies to get there were absolutely on-target. A tactical error had thrown him off course. While the check he held in his hands could improve the financial welfare of his business, thus taking him closer to his vision in some ways, it was also at odds with his vision AND his strategies.

Howard had not only neglected to share his vision (and the strategies) with his team in a meaningful way, he had not given them ethical guidelines. That resulted in his well-meaning top-selling agent relying on her own personal ethics. She truly felt she was doing the right thing by doing her best to keep her sales figures high.

Without the critical information hiding in Howard's vision and the essential logic behind the strategies he designed, the travel agent's tactical actions were left to chance. Now he faced an ethical choice that could change not only his own life, but also the lives of those who depended on him.

Howard did choose. He told me that it was one of the most difficult decisions of his life. He was well aware of all the things and all the people that would be affected by his choice. In the end, he chose from his heart. He chose by reconnecting with his vision - emotionally. He chose by reconnecting with his strategies – logically.

He chose by recognizing and understanding the tactical errors that resulted from his lack of ethical guidelines.

Howard chose to return the check.

Challenges

Before you define your own ethics, list some things that have been ethical challenges for you in the past. Try to think of those things that had an impact on the vision you now hope to bring to life.

_____

_____

_____

_____

_____

_____

_____

_____

_____

Your Ethics

Remember that the purpose of defining guiding principles is to help you with day-to-day decision making related to your vision. What is the *"right"* thing to do to create and sustain your vision?

_____

_____

_____

_____

_____

_____

_____

_____

_____

I have learned the most about integrity not from the times I had it, but from the times I lost it and experienced the consequences.

Integrity
The Succeeding Part

Success is not an event; it is an ongoing process. Throughout this book the word *"destination"* has been frequently used to represent the vision in reference to the journey we must take to get there.

What or where is *"there?"* It is the successful realization and manifestation of your vision! But, once you get *"there"* is it all over and done in a flash? Let's hope not.

Sometimes however, that is exactly how we behave. Once you get *"there"* don't you want to stay *"there?"* Maybe you even want to go beyond *"there"* to climb higher mountains, live bigger dreams and build grander visions than ever before. Whether the motivation is centered on the next vision or simply keeping the existing one alive and well, a little lesson in maintenance is in order.

Integrity like ethics is a powerful word. For some, these two words carry the same basic meaning. Ethics is a form of integrity and integrity is a form of ethics in some ways. There is another collection of meanings for the word integrity as it pertains to Visionistics. Think about the words *"integrated"* and *"integral."*

The word integrated refers to the coming together of various elements into a single unit of common purpose or direction. Any bit or piece that stands alone or in opposition is no longer integrated and threatens the stability of the unit. You might even say that the unit is at increased risk of collapse.

Integral refers to any element that is essential to the whole like a single gear among the dozens within a clock. Should any one gear fail or simply not be installed in the first place, the likelihood of proper timekeeping is almost nonexistent.

Integrity also means that you do what you say you're going to do and you are what you say you are. It is all part of an ongoing process. Visionistics is a process. It is a process that involves the integration of vision, strategies, tactics and ethics for the single purpose of success. Every element is integral to that success. If one gear fails or is not installed in the first place, the chances of success are greatly diminished.

When every gear is in place spinning in synchronized motion something wonderful happens. Each gear part is integrated into a single unit driving the second hand forward, which pushes the minute hand forward, which pushes the hour hand forward which moves the clock closer and closer to triggering the alarm that signals, success is here! It's a clever analogy because one second later it can all come to a screeching halt.

Integrity is about constant monitoring of every element to ensure synchronized movement toward the vision. Are the strategies still in sync with the vision? Things will surely change from time to time. What about the tactics? Are the ethical guidelines still intact and working? Are they all still in alignment or are they putting the stability of the unit at risk? Have any of them ventured so far from the vision that an entirely new vision has emerged?

That can happen too and it's not all bad. It is however a bit backwards. Vision comes from the heart. Strategies are the logical plans to make the vision come true. Tactics are the physical steps taken to support the strategies, which by extension support the vision. Ethics help you and others make the decisions needed for all of them! If any of the elements go so far out of alignment that the vision no longer rings true, it is clear evidence that the passion has faded so much that it can no longer outshine the gleaming distractions that have overtaken it.

The problem with a new vision resulting from distractions is that it will likely suffer the same fate. Wouldn't it be better to try to reconnect with the original vision in the same way it was created? If you can go back to that emotional place where dreams are born, where logic and physical limitations have not yet become a factor, you might rediscover the magic that inspired it all.

It is also possible that the vision of yesterday no longer agrees with the person or organization you have become. If you have evolved in a way that gives you happiness and joy then your new vision will be born of the right stuff.

You will probably also find though, that the original vision played a fairly important role in getting you to where you are. In other words, your original vision transformed into one of the strategies that put it on the new path. So perhaps it wasn't a failure or an extinguished vision after all. Maybe it was just another step on the grander journey you've yet to take. Only your heart can tell.

If your organization has grown or expanded in unexpected ways you may have a new vision in the works. If it is a new direction that still uplifts and serves your customers or employees then it may be worth reexamining the original vision. Perhaps it just needs a tweak or two or maybe a total replacement. Either way, as with the personal vision above it should at least be recognized as an important part of the journey to this moment.

A note of caution however: businesses and other organizations are in particular danger of what you might call *"continual vision replacement syndrome."* This is not necessarily bad but is usually the result of simple mathematics.

The original vision that started it all usually came from one single person's heart. It may have been shared with others to begin the building and creation process through strategies, tactics, ethics and integrity but it was still one person's vision.

That person and their vision are far outnumbered. The cacophony of *"yes but"* and *"I don't agree"* and *"why don't we try this way instead"* can easily overwhelm a quietly emotional vision. If the visionary is still around it's a little easier to keep turning up their own volume and reminding others of who is in charge. If however the visionary has long since moved along someone else will be manning the volume control.

This is why it is critically important for a business, or any other organization, to tread carefully before tossing an old vision out the window. The business landscape is littered with the ruins of failed ventures that completely turn their backs on the vision that made them possible. The best advice is to get to the core of the vision.

What was the fundamental meaning of the vision? Was it great service or was it all about value? Was it about innovation and creativity? Whatever the core of the vision was, it is still the best place to start when considering a new one.

Be it the journey of a vision held for years or a bright and shiny new one; integrity is the glue that will hold it all together. When all the elements are in alignment and everything is integrated and everything is integral, you have a state of integrity. It is from this state of being that success will almost naturally emerge.

Strategies

Vision · Ethics

Tactics

Howard's Story

Part Five

When Howard made the decision to return the check he had received for exceptional sales performance, he did it with confidence but with a self-admitted ounce of fear. His financial realities of the day would indicate that he was making a bad decision. The tour supplier to whom he returned the check thought it was an absolutely terrible decision! For Howard, it was the right decision.

Howard reconnected with his vision to share the beauty of planet earth with others through selling travel to his beloved magical destinations. His strategy of only supporting tour operators that shared his vision and helped to preserve those magical destinations was a strong and sound business strategy very much connected to his vision. His tactical error of selling the *"wrong"* supplier due to his lack of clear ethical guidelines could not be changed. But, he could make an ethical decision and change tactics for the future.

Howard not only returned the check with apologies and thanks to the supplier, he took a few other pretty dramatic steps. He sent a letter to every customer that had already purchased a trip using the supplier stating that his company had *"made a serious error that was not in alignment with our vision."* They offered to continue to provide support and assistance to any customer that wanted to go ahead with their plans to use the supplier. They also offered to give them a credit equal to any commissions they had earned as a result of the sale.

Howard then wrote another letter to customers who had already traveled using the supplier in the past saying basically the same thing. They offered those customers a credit on account equal to the past commission they had earned from the sale. The combined commission credits and the return of the $10,000 override bonus were significant enough to potentially bring an early end to Howard's dream.

But then, something almost unbelievable happened. As the many letters began to arrive in mailbox after mailbox his telephone started to ring. One after another, customer after customer called him to share their feelings. They said things like *"you are amazing"* and *"this is exactly why I am happy to do business with you"* and *"you have got a customer for life"* and *"I didn't know businesses like this still existed. Thank you for renewing my faith."*

Most of the callers flatly refused to accept Howard's offer to return or credit the commission he had earned. Most said they would prefer that he keep it. It was as if they were doing their own part in keeping his dream alive. Some may even have had similar dreams of their own.

Then another thing happened. Howard got a call from a newspaper reporter. Word had spread and a story followed. Before long Howard's dream was in overdrive. Eventually his agency was among the top agencies in town. Not long after that, it was among the leading agencies of his type in the nation.

Howard's success was at least in part the result of integrity. To be more specific, it was the result of getting his integrity back. It wasn't just the letters, or the apologies within them, or the offer of financial reward that did it. It was when ALL the elements of vision, strategies, tactics and ethics came into alignment that success emerged.

Howard and You

Take a moment to reflect on Howard's story and think about similar events in your own life or business. Can you recall instances where integrity and vision brought about positive change?

_____

_____

_____

_____

_____

_____

_____

_____

_____

The most important time to trust that everything will work out is when it seems that it won't. Having faith during good times alone isn't really faith at all.

Belief

The Trusting Part

Picture your vision at the very center of a seesaw. On one end of the seesaw is doubt and on the other is belief. The end that gets the most weight at any given time will cause your vision to slide in that direction. The nature of life is such that we may be continually moving from one dominant mindset to the other. The question is: on which side of the seesaw do you prefer to spend most of your time?

You might wonder why anyone would prefer to live a life of doubt and negativity but there is a curious reward to such an existence. Think about those who seem to light up with delight when they tell stories of their personal woes. Consider those who seem to get some satisfaction in telling others about all the things they've tried that didn't work out. Haven't we all known someone who retells the same story of despair over and over any chance they get? Haven't we all occasionally felt the urge to share our own personal problems or bad experiences from time to time?

Truly, it can sometimes feel good to talk about feeling bad! We all do it once in a while. But, if you spend too much of your time and energy talking about or reliving bad experiences or unpleasant circumstances you will be in danger of developing a habit of negativity. This is not to say that doubt is an entirely bad thing.

Belief is powerful. Doubt is powerful. Both serve useful purposes. Doubt encourages investigation and learning, where belief moves us forward toward new ideas and possibilities. Doubt is more about the current reality whereas belief is more about potential realities and can even be used to overcome the current reality. Overcome reality? Absolutely!

Gravity is real. Birds however believe and trust in their wings enough to overcome that reality and create a new reality of flying in spite of the existence of gravity. Injuries and accidents aside, falling only becomes a reality when they stop using the wings in which they trusted.

Doubt, like gravity is easy and reliable. Just let go, stop trying, stop believing and you'll fall flat every time. Giving up is a safe bet that never disappoints but also rarely satisfies.

If you want to create a new or different

reality for yourself, you will have to put forth some extra effort and flap your wings of belief. Belief is the place where your vision materializes and doubt is where (if you stay there too long) it withers and dies.

The steps leading from doubt to belief are really just varying degrees of confidence. Confidence is something you build step-by-step, thought-by-thought, action-by-action and experience-by-experience. Confidence is not something you just happen upon, nor is it something you are born with. Confidence is developed through a combination of the strength of your desire and learning from your mistakes. It also comes from the very essence of belief: commitment.

Belief, trust and faith are all expressions of confidence, certainty and commitment. These expressions apply to you as well. Faith in the religious sense often refers to the belief in a higher power. It may even mean placing one's trust in that higher power. This form of faith is beautiful yet externalized. What about belief, trust and faith in yourself? That form of faith may be a bit more difficult for some yet it is critically important.

A lack of faith in oneself is usually the cumulative result of past experiences and present circumstances. If you find yourself having difficulty believing in your own ability to succeed just remember that you are not trying to replicate the current reality but instead to create a new and different one. In that new and different reality the person you are or were is irrelevant. That new reality is all about the person you wish to become. Belief is the strength of your desire to become that person.

Are you on-target to achieving your visions? Are you moving closer to bringing your desires to life or are they slipping ever further away? Are your actions and decisions in alignment with your dreams? How do you know if you are moving in the right direction?

The answer to one simple question can reveal all of the above: *how do you feel?*

Belief is yet another emotional experience. As you've already read, emotions are very powerful things. Your emotional state is both a generator of change and a very efficient indicator of progress. Fear, desire, excitement, anger, stress, pleasure, pressure, anticipation, joy and many more are all examples of motivators that push us toward taking action. They also influence the ever-changing balance between belief and doubt.

Taking action also results in a range of potential emotions such as pride, regret, satisfaction, elation, and more. In an almost cyclical manner it is often the reaction to your action that will determine the next action you take!

Emotions are motivators AND indicators. Still, common logic may tell you that the way you feel is primarily a result of your present circumstances. In reality, the way you feel can completely change your circumstances! This is easier to understand when you compare pessimism to optimism.

A pessimist might say that his or her cautious, doubting mindset is a result of past failed attempts or bad experiences. Once pessimism becomes the prevailing attitude every subsequent feeling, thought, action or decision will be focused on failure or the expectation of more bad experiences. The outcome of any attempt to change built on a foundation of doubt and fear will very likely be more of the same. If pessimism is the starting place then disappointment will more often than not, be the end result – and the cycle continues.

You've probably heard the old expression *"hope for the best but expect the worst and you won't be disappointed."* Somehow, the *"hope"* that's mentioned in that saying doesn't seem to carry much weight. The intent to avoid disappointment is far stronger than any hope for the best.

Sometimes, as evident in this seemingly harmless saying, a pessimistic mindset is less about pure negativity and more about fear. Think again about those people you may know who seem to enjoy telling others about their never-ending problems. They may genuinely fear losing their identity as the one for whom nothing ever seems to work out!

An optimistic mindset is one of possibilities, excitement and yes, belief. Every feeling, thought, action or decision for an optimist is far less burdened by past experiences, even the bad ones. Disappointments of yesterday are seen as positive learning experiences and not just bitter reminders or justification for contempt.

Since the realization of your vision is so often directly or indirectly dependent upon others it isn't difficult to imagine how an optimistic attitude can be of benefit. You have to believe in the possibility of your own dreams and desires before you can expect anyone else to do the same and help you. Any fear or doubt that you feel will quickly spread to those around you. Your own optimism, excitement and belief on the other hand, will motivate and inspire others.

As you can see, belief is more than just trust or faith in yourself. Belief is more than positive thinking or hoping for the best. Belief is confidence and commitment acting like a magnet to attract others of similar vision or purpose. It is the transformative element that propels vision from your emotional heart and into your logical mind. It is the sculptor that carves your big picture strategies into perfectly executable tactics. It is the navigator that guides your ethics into place. Belief completes the circuit that allows your vision to flow into reality.

Without belief everything we imagine is little more than a daydream. With belief, our imagination becomes the creator of all our tomorrows.

Your Belief and Commitment

How confident are you in your vision? Does doubt or belief dominate your thoughts and feelings? Are you ready to commit?

I now commit my best thoughts, feelings and actions to the following:

_____

_____

_____

_____

_____

_____

_____

_____

Speak from your heart, act from your soul and live from your dreams.

Balance

The Maintenance Part

Success is indeed a process. It is not just an event that springs into existence and remains forever present. Success is an ongoing process that requires on-going maintenance. By understanding that success is more of an internal sense of satisfaction than the external judgment of others, the means of sustaining it become clear. You must look within.

Your visions, your dreams, your passions and all those other internal emotional experiences are at the very root of your sense of satisfaction. To once again reference Bill Gates, one might assume that the impressive financial accomplishments of Microsoft would be a fairly significant indicator of his success. While sales and profits may be a measure of the success of the business, his personal sense of satisfaction might be measured by something other than dollars and cents.

Only Mr. Gates knows how he feels about his many achievements. His long-held vision of a computer on every desk and in every home has become a reality in most businesses and in most homes. The satisfaction that arises from seeing that reality unfold may give him far greater joy than the financial rewards. Then again, the two may be intimately connected given his philanthropic endeavors.

Balance is crucial to sustaining any success that you may experience. Be it on a personal level or as a participant in a business, we must continually weigh our every thought, feeling and action against the vision. Are you moving closer to or further away from alignment with the vision? Even within the framework of vision, strategies, tactics and ethics there is a need to maintain balance.

Imagine a carpenter's bubble level. It is an exceedingly simple tool that registers the slightest shift in balance. When placed on a flat surface, a tilt in any direction will become instantly apparent as the tiny bubble moves from the center.

Now imagine placing the four fundamental elements of Visionistics around the level as pictured on the next page.

Strategies

Vision  Ethics

Tactics

As mentioned before, a vision that only lives in your heart is unlikely to materialize. Likewise giving all your attention to strategic or tactical issues will result in a lopsided foundation that is just as unlikely to result in success. Unlike the carpenter dealing with solid objects, which rarely move once set, life is in constant motion. A balanced life requires awareness of the ever-changing shifts we make in our day-to-day thoughts, feelings and actions.

In a business, one of the most common misalignments seems to occur at the tactical level where the employees may be the most separated from the vision and its intent. As you read in *Howard's Story* however, without fully integrated ethical guidelines tactical errors are almost certain to occur.

With a personal vision it is often the strategies that are most lacking. Many of us can dream big dreams but not everyone can make big plans. For some people the planning and idea making is the easy part but taking the tactical steps to actually do something can be difficult.

None of these elements should stand in isolation. They are all equally important in creating the state of integrity from which success can emerge and thrive.

How do you know when you are out of balance? How do you know when you are out of integrity? We all have a built-in bubble level that can register the subtle and not-so-subtle shifts in balance. The indicators go by many names such as guilt, stress, resentment, remorse, sadness and a host of other emotional maladies. Just as pain can alert you to potential bodily damage, unpleasant emotions alert you to potential dream damage.

Curiously some very pleasant emotions can also throw a success story out of balance. Think about how excited and invigorated we can become when something new and different competes for our attention. The lure of something fresh can cause boredom to set in and negatively impact a dream in incubation.

How can you offset shifts in balance and maintain the integrity of your vision? Remember to weigh each thought, feeling and action against its potential to take you closer to your vision. How does it feel? Does it logically agree with your vision? Is it about doing things that are aligned with your vision? Is it related to your vision at all or is it an entirely new yet complimentary vision in the making?

Be aware of anything that is in opposition to your vision. Otherwise, a shift in balance and collapse of integrity could be the result. This is where dreams fall apart and businesses fail. But, even if such a collapse should happen, complete recovery is always possible. That is the truly beautiful thing about a vision that comes from your heart. It is always waiting for you to reconnect and reignite the passion that started it all.

Vision is the feeling part.
Strategies are the thinking part.
Tactics are the doing part.
Ethics are the guiding part.
Integrity is the succeeding part.
Belief is the trusting part.
Balance is the maintenance part.

Isn't it time to bring all the parts together and watch your every dream unfold? Isn't it time to reexamine your business or professional life and find or reignite the passion that put you there in the first place? If there is no passion left, then isn't it time to find it somewhere else?

There are infinite amounts of joy and satisfaction to be experienced but a finite amount of time to make the journey. The journey can begin at any moment. It will begin the moment you decide to take the first step and look inside. Somewhere in your heart there is a vision, a dream or an idea that is waiting to be born.

You can make it happen by remembering where it all began and where it will eventually return. It starts, ends and is continually reborn within you. Isn't that the most magical part of all?

Success is a process. It is driven by vision, fuelled by passion and sustained by integrity. We call this process Visionistics.

About the Author
Nolan W. Burris

For some people, the term *"poor white trash"* makes them think of trailer parks, big hair and monster trucks. For Nolan Burris something else comes to mind: roots.

Growing up in Oklahoma, poor and spending years living in an aluminum-clad tornado target can teach you a lot. For Nolan it was the perfect beginning of a life filled with adventure and exploration.

Nolan is an author, former travel agent, failed musician and self-professed techno-geek. He's also an in-demand international speaker. He travels around the world teaching others how to create success in their own lives and businesses.

He is the founder of Visionistics Enterprises, based in Vancouver, Canada. He formed Visionistics with the idea that if you can change the way business works, you will change the world. His belief in the power of integrity goes beyond the confines of business and is fundamental in his approach to life. His vision is to spread the transformative magic of integrity, ethics and human compassion in a technology-driven world.

Would you like to learn more?

Visionistics was born from the experience of witnessing ordinary people and everyday businesses reshape their realities. Through the alignment of passion, thought and action guided by ethics, a state of integrity emerged to make their hopes and dreams possible. What about yours?

Visionistics Enterprises and Nolan Burris regularly conduct workshops and seminars on applying the principles you've learned in this book. Nolan is also a featured speaker at conferences and conventions around the world.

You may contact us through our website at **www.visionistics.com**. We would love to hear from you.

If you are interested in having Nolan Burris speak at a conference or convention, you can learn more on his speaker's website at **www.nolanburris.com**.